Traders Remember Deal and Walmer

Harry Williams with his children Ann and John in the doorway of the family shop at 78 College Road, Deal, in 1959.

Bygone Publishing

A catalogue record for this book is available from the British Library

ISBN 978-0-9566172-1-7

Printed and bound in Great Britain by Geerings of Ashford

Front cover shows a queue of diners outside Catt's Restaurant in King Street, Deal, c1950.

Also by Judith Gaunt:
Shops Remembered in Deal and Walmer (2009)
Basil's Deal: Pictures from Basil Kidd's Photographic Archive (2010)

Dedication

In memory of Helen

Contents

Introduction

This is the long awaited companion to my first album, Shops Remembered in Deal and Walmer. It quickly became clear while writing that book there would be enough material for a second – and since then several people have kindly offered me more photographs.

This time, I decided I wanted to record the stories and photographs of other businessmen and women of the town, not just shopkeepers, so, again, a second volume would be the answer.

The book includes a variety of shops not featured in my previous book along with a reminder of the garages, hairdressers, chimney sweeps, market gardeners and many more traders who have helped supply and serve the people of Deal and Walmer over the centuries.

The layout of Traders Remembered in Deal and Walmer echoes that of Shops Remembered. It starts in Beach Street, follows along College Road, Alfred Square, through the High Street to Broad Street and Queen Street, past the southern section of the High Street, to Victoria Road, on towards Walmer and Upper Walmer and Upper Deal.

I have also included a section, Around the Town, which takes in some other businesses.

Finally, remembering there was a small army of errand boys and delivery men ensuring the goods reached their customers, I have included a section devoted to them and their various modes of transport.

Judith Gaunt
Deal, Kent
October 2012

Prince of Wales Terrace & "Channel View" Nursing Home, Deal

Beach Street – At the mention of the Pegasus Restaurant people will often say: "Egg and chips on a Saturday night." Joyce and Ivor Griffiths ran the business from around 1959 to 1971. In 1987 Ian Dunkerley purchased the property for his restaurant, extending into The Pier Hotel 10 years later. The building is pictured as the Imperial Restaurant, which preceded Pegasus Restaurant. Around 1936, Frederick East had run the business and before that it was Achille Mangilli's Grand Café and Restaurant.

Joyce Griffiths (centre) relaxing with her sister Beryl and brother-in-law John Martin after readying Pegasus Restaurant for its first day of business at the end of the 1950s. With little money for furnishings they painted the chairs various colours, added checked tablecloths and created one of the most popular cafés in Deal of its time.

Pegasus Restaurant waitresses, in their blue gingham aprons, pause for a photocall on Deal Pier in 1962. Left to right are: Eve Trice, Mary Johnson, Dorothy Jackson, Anthea Johnson daughter of the owner, Iris Fagg and Joyce Griffiths, owner of the business.

Above: Tony Divito stands at the window of the Divito Bros ice cream counter selling 'The softa ice that's twice as nice.' Divito Bros traded further along Beach Street but this outlet was ideal for tempting customers in the more central area opposite Deal Pier. Inset: Tony's wife Barbara stands at the counter of the premises before modernisation.

A bustling Deal seafront with sunbathers, deckchairs and the working fishermen and boats that once graced this area. In the row of shops in the background is Solley's Dairy which later became Duncan's Fishing Tackle shop. Alongside is William Humfrey's chemist that was later taken over by Mr C Harbron and then became Lewis the Chemist. Opposite is King's toy and fancy goods shop that was previously the East India Arms public house.

Day trippers, the women in their fancy hats, photographed before taking advantage of the 'circular drive' tour of the local area. Just behind is a local postman in his distinctive hat and men with a horse and cart. The picture gives a closer view of Solley's Dairy, pictured on the previous page but shown here as Mongeham Farm Dairy, and Humfrey's chemist next door. A local boatman surveys the scene from the window of the old Boatmen's Rooms.

Staff of Mongeham Farm Dairy, Great Mongeham (Deal depot), proudly pose for a photograph. Centre, between two impressive milk churns inscribed with the name of the firm, is Will Kemp. Solleys, who owned the dairy shop, still farm at Great Mongeham and produce ice cream at Ripple. They were established in 1854 and could boast Deal and Walmer Castles, the Admiralty and many hotels among their customers.

Above: A group of local businessmen out for a day's fishing pose for the photographer. Left to right are thought to be: William R Turk, local watchmaker of 76 High Street, Claude Darracott, jeweller of 60 High Street, Ernest Voizey, butcher of Alfred Square and Ald Sidney Pittock JP of John Pittock & Son drapers and outfitters, 49-53 High Street.

Left: A lucky angler proudly holds up his 40lb cod for a Basil Kidd photograph outside Duncan Finn's fishing tackle shop, formerly Solley's Dairy. Sharp's Dairy took over the premises and had the town's first milk vending machine outside, which can just be seen on the left of this picture. More recently Nicole Loftus-Potter ran Decores antique shop here.

Divito Bros ice cream parlour, a much loved favourite in the town, was located at the corner of Chapel Street. The familiar Lloyd Loom wicker chairs can be seen through the window and, to the right, the window for the takeaway ice cream trade. The premises had earlier been Henry Larkin's fishmongers and, before being converted to a house, was for a while the Flying Dutchman Restaurant.

A young Jane Divito in charge of the toy ice cream van outside Divito Bros ice cream parlour with Tony Divito standing at the takeaway ice cream window.

A behind the counter view of Divito Bros ice cream parlour.

Above: The choc-ice making machine in the ice cream factory behind Divito Bros.

Right: Lawrence Divito at work in the ice cream factory.

The di Vito family, as the name was originally spelt, moved to Deal from Scotland but had originally come to this country from Italy. Standing centre are Antonina and Antonio Divito with children John, left, and right George and Tony. In the front are Horace, Jean and Lawrence. John, Tony and Lawrence went on to run the Divito Bros business.

26366. DEAL. THE PARADE. JUDGES' LTD.

This picture shows the row of shops immediately alongside Divito Bros opposite The Royal Hotel. On the left, at 95 Beach Street, is the Tudor Galleries owned by Mrs Norah Remes who rented out the apartments above. Joan Wright ran the premises for many years as The Print Room. On the right, at number 97, was Ling's Café owned by Fred Ling who was famous for taking a dip in the sea every morning at 6.55am.

The stretch of Beach Street, north of The Royal Hotel, shows Desormeaux hairdressers at 125 Beach Street, just before the Three Compasses public house. The 1911 census lists Thomas Desormeaux, hairdresser, at the property. Thomas was born in Spitalfield, London, and lived with his wife Sarah, their son Arthur, aged 23, and widowed daughter Laura Jarratt, aged 43. Thomas also appears to have run The Harp public house in Middle Street, now Middle Street Fish Bar.

John Pierce Catt's café at 171
Beach Street, now a private
house, pictured about 1920.
Left to right are Emma Roberts,
who married Charles Catt;
Winnie Catt half sister of John
Pierce Catt; John Pierce Catt
and his wife Harriet and a
young helper. Catt's Restaurant,
at its more familiar location in
King Street, is featured later in
this book.

Stan Langridge stands with the cars he has cleaned at the new North Deal Garage showroom for a Basil Kidd photograph around 1963. The garage was owned by Sidney Lawrence Cookman and earlier by motor engineers Trollope and Rivers. North Deal Garage was at 5-6 The Marina, approached via a narrow access; the showroom pictured was in Sandown Road. Both locations are now the site of housing and the business later became part of Campbell's Garage. Layton's Garage, featured in the advertisement on the right, was also on The Marina, now at numbers 21-24.

Sandown Road – East Kent Mercury editor Robin Brazier releases balloons at Sandown Garage, as part of a promotion to 'Test drive the new Renault Trafic T800,' launched in 1980. Lead's promotional bus is on the right and was formerly owned by Thomsett's Coaches. The garage, established by Dennis Percy Lead, was situated at the corner of Sandown and Harold Roads but was demolished and replaced by houses when the firm relocated to Dover. Earlier, Captain S Claydon ran a garage on the site listed as Claydon's Garage but also called Harold Road Garage.

College Road – Knowles Foodmarket was a very popular shop in College Road near the corner of Ark Lane. The business was started as a cake and sweet shop around 1920 by Harry and Ivy Knowles in a property on the opposite side of College Road before the shop pictured was built. Later, the business was taken over by their son Roy and family. Roy, pictured inset, was President of the Deal and Walmer Chamber of Trade for three years from 1977-79. In 1979 Chris Gray and his wife Roberta took over the business before returning to the building industry with CJ Gray Builders. The Khan family took on the shop but sadly in 1995 the property was undermined following Southern Water sewerage works which caused subsidence. It was finally demolished and is now houses.

Alfred Square – In 1954 a series of events was organised around the town to promote forthcoming films at the Odeon Cinema in Queen Street, photographed by local firm Chapman and Day. This view of Alfred Square shows advertising for Susan Slept Here, a romantic comedy starring Debbie Reynolds, hence the bed in the foreground. Luckily two shops are captured beyond, Georgie Bishop's men's hairdressers and North Deal Wool Shop run by Mrs Town.

High Street – Basil Kidd's photograph shows the lower end of Deal High Street with a flourishing array of businesses including the popular Thompson's Large Dustpan Stores on the far left. The property on the corner of Ivy Place, at 172, was for decades a branch of Jennings & Co butchers but at the time of the photograph was W Drew's fruit shop. Alongside was a sweet shop and next door at 168, Stephen Laker had earlier had his bookshop, see overleaf. In the foreground is the land cleared for road widening in 1962 that had been the site of Clarence House (see inset) home of the Whitlock family and their horticultural nursery. RG Whitlock, a son of the owner, took over the business and the shop frontage was at 183 High Street. Clarence Place, the neo-Georgian terrace of houses, now stands on the site.

Stephen Laker's bookshop at 168 High Street is gaily decked out to celebrate the Silver Jubilee of King George V and Queen Mary in 1935. Stephen Laker, pictured above, was born at 94 Middle Street, the son of a bootmaker. He became an apprentice printer for the Deal Mercury before opening his shop where he had a lending library and sold newspapers. Earlier, around 1911, John and Evelyn Coleman were newsagents at the premises. More recently, the premises housed Serendipity antiques and is now a secondhand bookshop.

This Basil Kidd picture shows the stretch of Deal High Street shops opposite what is now the Union Road car park which was created by the demolition, for road widening, of David Parkin's Garage and the Queen's Arms public house. In the row of shops at the corner of New Street, was Denne's seed merchants which later became Channel Wines and is now Blind Illusions. Next was The Olde Forge, RT Baker & Son shoe shop and, on the corner of Farrier Street, old Mrs Smith's secondhand shop. Hogden's furniture shop came next followed by Snuff, Puff and Candy tobacconist and sweet shop that had earlier been McManus's and before that run by Alex King.

Now the site of Union Road Car Park this Basil Kidd photo shows David Parkin Motors Ltd that was previously Handford Motors (Deal) Ltd and before that Crump's Garage. The Queen's Arms public house was to the right of the garage. The large Georgian house behind the garage has 'Worsfold and Hayward Auction Rooms' written on the façade, the firm were auctioneers and estate agents of Queen Street. The building was previously St Andrew's Rectory and one of several historic buildings demolished in the town.

We briefly divert to Farrier Street to a view that looks back across Middle Street towards the garage in the High Street, pictured opposite. On the left of the picture is the Deal Lugger off licence and general stores, known locally as Alloway's after the name of the owners. On the corner of Farrier Street, at 119 Middle Street, the doorway of a former shop can be seen set at an angle. Before World War Two this property was James Shaw's café, shown overleaf.

James Harold Shaw stands outside his tripe shop at 119 Middle Street, on the corner of Farrier Street, with his daughters Eileen and Kathleen. James and his wife worked long hours selling tripe, pork pies and meats, even working on Sundays serving everything from early morning cups of tea, to luncheons and suppers 'in a large room upstairs'. The pictures were taken about 1937-39 but the business was interrupted by the start of World War Two and never reopened, though the family continued to live at the property until around 1961.

A covering of snow decorates Ernest Duncan Newing's cycle shops at 138 and 140 High Street. The shops, which also sold radios and gramophones, are now Carried Away and the Deal Christian Resource Centre.

Above: Duncan Frederick Newing stands in the doorway of number 138. Duncan died, aged 22, only 10 months after father Ernest and the firm was then run by Duncan's younger brother, John, until he retired in 1974.

Mention the old shops at the north end of Deal High Street and many people will recall old Mrs Smith who seemed always to be standing in the doorway of her gradually dilapidating secondhand shop that was at the corner of Farrier Street. Eventually, the building became unsafe and had to be demolished. The land stood empty for many years until a house was built on the site. Bert Smith, Mrs Smith's husband, worked as a porter for the auction house opposite.

Mrs Ratliff, pictured here with her husband, was an earlier trader at the corner property featured in the previous picture. Mrs Ratliff ran her wardrobe dealer's business around 1924, 'wardrobe' being the term commonly used for clothing dealers selling and buying secondhand garments.

William Spicer, on the right in the striped apron, and his son Albert, on the left, are pictured in 1904 with an impressive display of meat at their pork butcher's shop at 134 High Street. The Spicer family, who lived across the road at number 149, had a long history in the butchery trade in Deal, the firm being established in 1850. Carriages could also be hired at the High Street shop, as the advertising board shows, and the young man in the shop doorway was possibly the driver. The shop became Maxted's pet shop before that business moved next door to number 136 and is now Joanne Harmer's Gallery.

In the picture on the previous page is Spicer's pork butchers of 134 High Street displaying an advertising board for carriage hire "Close or open carriages by the day or hour on most reasonable terms." The treasured family picture on this page shows one of the firm's carriages with 'Grandma Spicer' on the right holding baby Albert.

Fred Hutton owned Hutton's Dairy at 132 High Street and it was run by Doris Carpenter. Fred started as a milkman and later had his dairy and milk delivery business at Great Mongeham. When Fred sold up, the shop was renamed The Old Dairy and was owned by Miss Morris with Mrs Streeting as manageress. She continued as manageress when J&E Rogers of Church Path Bakery had the business until Celia Clayton took over the role. For many years before Fred Hutton had the premises it was JT Rogers' general store, featured on the front cover of the author's first book, *Shops Remembered in Deal and Walmer*, and it is now Delpierre Antiques.

A view of A Moffat's Bespoke Tailor that was at 130 High Street. The premises and next door at 128 High Street were formerly a branch of The World Stores Limited, with another branch at Mill Hill, and now forms the Pilgrims Hospices shop. The word 'World' is still to be seen on the entrance floor. Prior to The World Stores, around 1916, RJ Collett provisions dealer was in business here.

High Street, Deal.

121244.

A view of Deal High Street with the spires of the Congregational Church, now the Landmark Centre, clearly visible on the left. Extreme left is glimpsed the fine wrought iron balcony of 117 High Street which became The Christian Bookshop. Beyond is the Singer Sewing Machine shop and Alfred Simmonds jeweller. The property next along became the popular Japp's sweet shop and tobacconist owned by Mr and Mrs GF Japp. On the right was Sam's Place, an Italian ice cream parlour that became the Enterprise Leather Shop run by SR Baker. Next was Nash and Co fruiterer which had been Fletchers' butcher's shop and is now Jenkins and Son fishmongers.

Left: This view of Deal High Street, immediately beyond the Town Hall, shows the Black Bull public house, now Peppers health food shop. Next door was The Christian Bookshop with the fine wrought iron balcony that is still in place today. Mr and Mrs Kenneth Woods took over the business from Mr and Mrs Reynolds in 1956 who had taken on the lease in 1953 following the death of Mrs Green.

In 1969 Mr Woods moved the stationery side of the firm across the road to 104 High Street where Pearks grocery store had closed its doors for the last time. That stationery business eventually became Tyler's which closed in January 2012. Right: The shop frontage of The Christian Book Shop.

A young David Chamberlain stands outside Duncan Finn's fishing tackle shop holding his latest catch of a bass. The picture was taken by Duncan around 1962 when David, who is now a local marine researcher and author, was working in the shop. The premises were formerly Arthur Simmond's jeweller and the word 'engraving' is still written on the floor of the shop doorway. Miss Emily Dunn's secondhand furniture shop, was at the property at the time of the 1911 census. The shop is now Halo hairdressers.

Alongside Duncan Finn's Fishing Tackle shop at 125 High Street was the very popular sweet shop, pictured here in 1991, run by Mr and Mrs GF Japp. The business was previously Telling's sweet shop and in 1911 Richard Collett was a grocer here, with his daughter Mary, aged 14, assisting in the business. Until recently, Serendipity Antiques was at the premises and it is now Miretti Italian Patisserie.

Across the High Street from the previous four pictures is an early view of Charlie Jenkins in his family fishmongers Jenkins & Son at 118 High Street. Charlie had operated from his shop in Queen Street (see page 86) but joined his son Steve who had bought the High Street shop which had been a fishmonger's since 1929 and was owned by H Seath. Charlie has retired now and Steve continues to run the business.

This is an intriguing old photograph, thought to date from World War One, taken from the first floor of the Town Hall or neighbouring property opposite. There is a fireman in brass helmet in the centre of the picture but, as the fire engines were housed under the Town Hall at the time, that may not be significant. Whatever the event, the photograph is a superb record of the shops in the picture. On the left is 118 High Street as WR Fletcher butchers which is now Jenkins and Son fishmongers. Next door at 116 was James Charles White, stationer, paperhanger and picture framer. There is a glimpse of the initial 'N' of Nethersole's wine merchants on the right.

This photograph is of the depository and wine vaults of Castle & Co Limited wine merchants in the High Street, opposite the Town Hall. The company had a retail shop that was alongside the depository on the corner of Oak Street. Nethersole & Son Limited, established in 1802, previously traded on the site. Later, the building became derelict but was restored as an indoor market before being opened as Make Music piano, organ and musical instrument shop by Mr and Mrs Duke. More recently, the ground floor and cellars have been used as a variety of restaurants.

The smart frontage of Castle and Co wine merchants at the corner of Oak Street and the High Street was photographed by Basil Kidd in the early 1960s. The premises had previously been Nethersole & Son Limited, wine merchants and later became Barnardo's charity shop before being opened as the clothing boutique Noir.

Basil Kidd's atmospheric night time photograph of Castle & Co wine merchants on the corner of Oak Street and the High Street. The wrought iron shutters, pushed back during the day, are firmly closed for security.

ESTABLISHED 1802.

TELEPHONE No. 89.

Deal, *May. 1ˢᵗ 1925*

Mr. J. Arnold.

(Opposite Town Hall)

Victoria Rd.

Bot. of *Nethersole & Sons,* Deal. LIMITED.

IMPORTERS OF FOREIGN WINES AND SPIRITS.

Casks & Bottles, if not returned within 6 months, to be paid for.

S. T. Northey, Steam Printer, Deal.

1925.					
April 1st	To	a/c Rendered.		7	2	6
	—	Ale.		—	18	—
			£	8	—	6

Received Payment

For Nethersole & Sons Ltd.

With Compliments.

E. & O.E.

This is a view of the High Street just beyond the junction with Oak Street, opposite St George's Church and The Rose Hotel. Pearks grocery store, which closed in 1969 to become Deal's Bookshop, is on the left. Inside, there were glass counters each side and at the rear of the grocery shop. The staff would walk around them to collect goods requested by the customer, such as loose biscuits and slices from blocks of cheese and cakes. Next door in this picture is Stewart Dunn & Son chemist and photographic developers.

Vye & Son, previously Pearks, closed in 1969 and the premises became Deal's Bookshop, owned by Mr Kenneth Woods who had moved the stationery side of the business from The Christian Bookshop across the road at 117 High Street. In 1971 Denis Weaver Limited acquired the firm and retained Mr Woods as manager. Paul and Jill Tyler bought the business in 1987 but retired and closed the business in January 2012.

Stan Langridge, featured in the picture of North Deal Garage on page 21, had purchased an old Ford which he decorated and used for weddings. The photograph of the car parked outside St George's church gives an excellent view of the shops in the rear of the picture including Pearks, which became Vye & Son grocers, Stewart Dunn & Son chemist and Miss Ester Miles' florist.

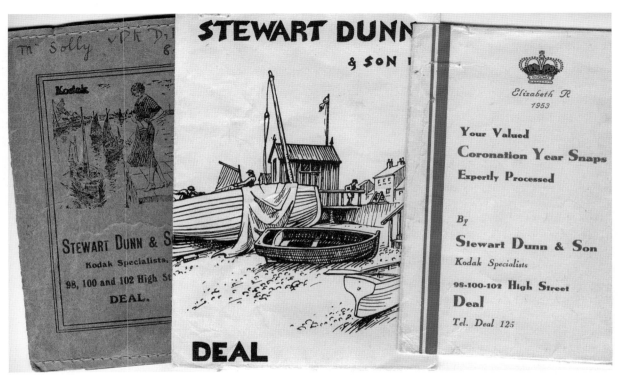

George Stewart Dunn opened his chemist shop at 98-102 High Street, shown on the opposite page, in 1885. His son, Ald Sidney Stewart Dunn, who was Mayor of Deal in 1956 and 1957, joined and later took over the firm. Around 1926 Ald Dunn started up Stewart Dunn & Sons photographic developers which would become a major employer in the town and pioneers of colour photography. The colour department was in the former Feed My Lambs' building in Middle Street. Eventually, the firm was sold to Colourcare International and moved to premises in Northwall Road. Shown here are three examples of the firm's photographic wallets, including an early one on the left and another celebrating the Coronation of Queen Elizabeth II in 1953 on the right.

A line-up of some of the staff of Stewart Dunn & Son photographic developers, dated February 1971. The group is standing in the firm's canteen, which was on the first floor at the rear of their High Street premises overlooking Middle Street. The canteen included a piano where the girls would practise routines for their staff parties – the colour processing staff against the black and white photography staff. On the wall on the left is a picture of the owner of the firm Ald Sidney Stewart Dunn in his mayoral robes.

An early picture, by photographers Franklin & Son of 3 High Street, taken in the garden of St George's Church, records the newly erected memorial to the dead of World War One. In the background is a gas lamp at the entrance to St George's Passage and, to the right, Jesse Springett Huntley's furniture and drapery store. The premises became Gordon Blain's bakery and greengrocers which were bombed and destroyed on 22 October 1942. Four people died in the shop with 16 more killed in the immediate area. For many years the site was Layton's Garage before the John Tapping Centre was built in 1989.

How beautiful Deal High Street looked in this picture when it could boast many ornate buildings with attractive awnings and features. To the left is 92-93 High Street, illustrated in the previous picture, and this time shows the magnificent cupola which dominated the landscape before being destroyed by World War Two bombing. Next door was Sylvester Eastes outfitters, Head's chemist that became the much loved Cox the Chemist and is now Seasons Café. To the right of the opening to St George's Hall, was Frederick Lass pastry cook and baker, established in 1828. The property is now A Stitch in Time wool and craft shop.

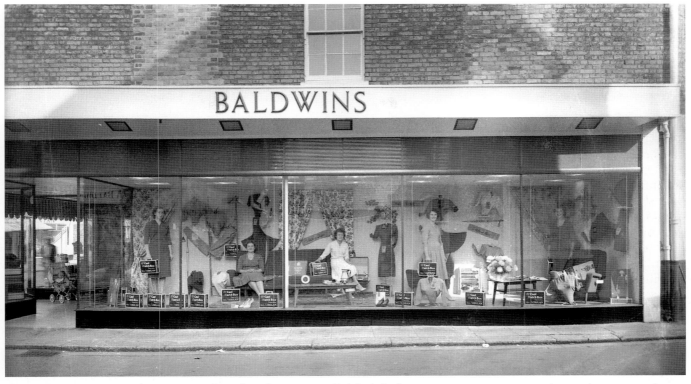

At 78 High Street, on the corner of Market Street, was Baldwin's department store, opened as a drapers and milliners by Theophilus Collins Baldwin in 1874 and still sadly missed. This picture was taken of the side window in Market Street and the supposed mannequins are actually staff. The business became Avora, then Superdeal, then Laughton's before finally closing in 2008, echoing the decline of department stores across the country. Laughton's removed to small premises behind the HSBC Bank in the High Street but finally closed in April 2012. The original Baldwin's site is now a branch of The Original Factory Shop.

"Are they real?" Bemused shoppers standing in Market Street look at a fun 1960s view of Baldwin's Department store window displaying some of the goods on sale while some of the staff model the latest outfits.

A spring fashion show at Baldwin's department store attracted the more mature ladies of the town.

William Hunnisett's 'fancy drapers' was at 70 High Street between Market Street and King Street. The premises, which had been Deal's original Town Hall, became an annexe of Baldwin's department store, pictured overleaf.

A view of 70 High Street, pictured opposite, as Baldwin's annexe, housing the china department. Later, the premises became Joyce Heath's china and glass shop but originally had been Deal's town hall.

Deal Motor Company showrooms and garage were on the corner of Stanhope Road. Southern Autos were at the premises before and, as the advertisement shows, Barnett & Co traded there even earlier. To the left can be glimpsed the striped blind of Dewhursts' butcher's shop, now part of JC Rook & Sons. People seldom look up to see the original Georgian property that is still visible above the shop frontages and was the home of Daniel Mackintosh Hills, head of Messrs Hills and Son, owners of the Deal Brewery. On the pathway, to the right of the picture, is a stack of boxes outside Cyril Williams' greengrocer.

Market Street/King Street – In 1906 John Pierce Catt opened a small pie shop in Middle Street, moving to slightly larger premises at 121 Middle Street. In 1912 he moved to 171 Beach Street (see page 20) before moving to Market Street. John's four sons Charles, George, Frank and Harry joined the family firm and then took over the business in 1952 when their father died. George is pictured in the doorway of the shop at 7a Market Street. The occasion was possibly the Coronation of George VI in 1937. The building had formerly been the Druids Arms public house and was destroyed in 1944 during World War Two bombing.

After World War Two Catt's Restaurant moved around the corner to King Street, on the corner of Middle Street, and the family lived above the premises. As the queues show, Catt's Restaurant was, and remained until its closure in 1969, much loved by the people of Deal. It is the King Street premises that are remembered with such affection, especially for the fish & chips and meat pies. It is still missed today.

Gradually the Catt's Restaurant premises expanded and this picture shows the extension to the restaurant on their former bombed site. Later, a first floor would be added to the extension, scene of many birthday parties, annual dinners and other functions.

ICES

Vanilla,
Strawberry

WONDER CAKE 8d.

Coffee,
Neopolitan
6d. & 1/-

PRALINE BOMBE 1/-

COLD SWEETS, SUNDAES, Etc.
as listed on our Luncheon Menu

COLD BEVERAGES
FRUIT SQUASHES
Orange, Lemon, Grapefruit, per glass 4d.

MINERALS
Orange, Lemon, Grapefruit, Vimto,
Ginger Beer, Kitty Kola, 6d.

LUCOZADE, 9d.　　　Leneys SHANDY GAFF. 7d
CHANDY. 7d.

WHITEWAYS CYDRAX, 6d.
Leneys Ginger Wine, 8d.

COLD or HOT MILK, per glass 5d.

The busy kitchens of Catt's Restaurant and, inset, an ices and cold drinks menu for the restaurant – fruit squash was 4d per glass, Vimto 6d and shandy 7d.

Right: The first floor of Catt's Restaurant, set out for a busy day's trading but the area would be transformed for evening events. The floor is now the Royal British Legion club.

Left: The ground floor of Catt's Restaurant with the familiar tables and chairs. The premises are now a Barnardo's charity shop.

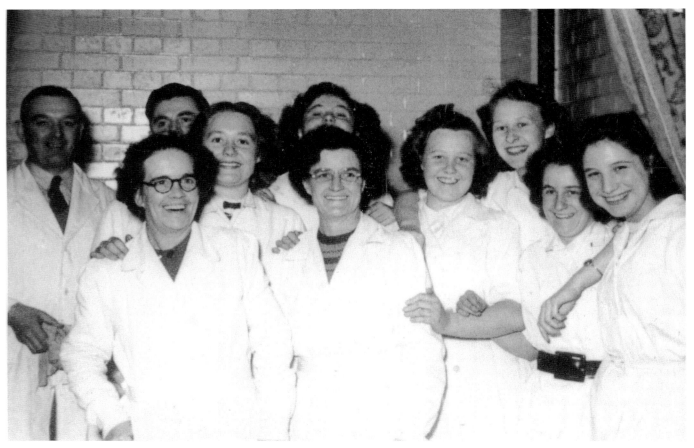

Members of the Catt family, their wives and other staff. How hard they worked. Left to right: Charles, Emma and George Catt, Daphne Sheldon, Dorothy, Louie Chandler, Cynthia Walton, Hazel Tonks, Evelyn Chandler and Emily.

A further view of King Street in the early 1960s, once again capturing Catt's Restaurant, also shows, right foreground, Castle and Co wine merchants. Next door is Little Billingsgate fishmongers and the newsagent on the corner which was owned by the Ferguson family at that time.

AW Bailey stands outside his butcher's shop on the corner of King Street and Middle Street, the shop bicycle ready for deliveries and the windows showing the style of ventilation of the period. Earlier, the business had been Frederick Jennings' Central Meat Stores and even earlier, Deal's first Post Office. More recently it was a branch of Elms Vale Cleaners and in December 2011 opened as The Just Reproach, Deal's first micro pub.

A closer view of AW Bailey's shop window display including meat on sale for 2s 8d and a pair of old style scales. The photograph was one of a series taken by local photographers Chapman and Day to promote the Odeon Cinema in 1954 when the poster on the right of the window was for the film Johnny Dark, starring Tony Curtis.

High Street cont – The street is in festive mode at the junction with King Street. On the right is the outfitters and drapery business of Thomas Stead Francis that became Brown's, featured on page 72, and beyond is Hunnisett's drapers. On the left, just beyond the junction with Park Street, is Freeman Hardy and Willis shoe shop. An assistant from the shop watches the photographer along with the staff of the Maypole Dairy next door in their long white aprons.

The first and second floor architecture is little changed now from when it was photographed here as the outfitters and linen drapery business of Thomas Stead Francis at 64-68 High Street. Part of the business became Brown's department store, later Brown and Phillips when Vivian Phillips took over the firm. The premises on the corner became White Fuller (Kent) Limited and is now Biggs Opticians.

A photograph taken in 1935 of Brown's department store at 60-64 High Street, following alteration of the shop front by Pike-Wootton of Ramsgate. The upper floors retain some of the features of the earlier building when owned by outfitter and draper Thomas Stead Francis and pictured on page 71. The business became Brown and Phillips when Vivian Phillips bought the firm in 1938 and is now a branch of Savers.

The splendid and popular sight of the band of the Royal Marines as it leads a parade through Deal High Street photographed by Basil Kidd. On the left is a later view of the premises featured on page 70. Mount's Farm Shop had taken over the premises of Pilcher and Chittenden greengrocers in the early 1970s and is now a branch of the Halifax. Freeman Hardy and Willis shoe shop is next door, now Zoom Photos. On the right is a shop sign for Currys electricals, and Bata's shoe shop is beyond, on the corner of Custom House Lane.

This view of the High Street is a little further along than the previous picture. On the right, at 44 High Street, can be seen John Woodruff's family butcher's, which became Peter Harris Mayes' butcher's – 'Deal with Mayes it pays' – and is now a branch of Clark's shoe shop. Next door was the International Stores which became Walter & Son shoe shop and is now Costa Coffee. Henry Frost's ironmonger's is alongside with the distinctive gas lamps outside. On the left is a view of John Pittock's outfitters and drapers, with Freeman Hardy and Willis shoe shop in the distance.

Frost's ironmongers was at 54 High Street, run by Henry Gandar Frost. It later became Thomas Tapper's and the foundry to the business was in Custom House Lane behind the High Street shop. Later, the premises were a branch of the Scotch Wool Shop.

An internal view of the foundry of Henry Frost's ironmongers giving an idea of the vast variety of goods, from knives to fancy scrollwork, that could be made on the premises and sold in the firm's High Street shop.

Victor Value was one of, if not the first, self-service grocery shops in Deal. Later it became part of Tesco and the business moved to Queen Street. The premises are now a branch of Nationwide Building Society. To the right was the Westminster Bank, now Holland and Barrett. To the left was Goulden & Wind music shop. All three were built on the site of three original shops which were bombed on 11 October 1940. Out of view on the right of the picture is the Black Horse Hotel which became The Strand public house.

HIGH STREET, DEAL.

35610 JV

This picture is taken immediately south of The Black Horse Hotel and shows Ernest Hardy's newsagent and stationer alongside. Samuel Thomas Northey's printers, booksellers, stationer, bookbinder, newsagent and fancy goods dealer is pictured across the road next door to Clarabut's department store. Northey's moved into Hardy's premises and the business was later purchased by John Roper – and still trades under that name today. Roper's extended into the shop next door that had been Merrygarden's Florist which moved to 96 High Street c1987.

High Street, Deal.

A similar view to the previous picture but this time showing the smart art deco style of the Burton's tailors' logo. The policeman stands at the junction which is wonderfully devoid of vehicles, traffic lights and with minimal road markings. On the right of the picture is a glimpse of the fancy wrought iron sign of Timothy White's the chemist.

The magnificient sight of the band of the Royal Marines parading through Deal was photographed by Basil Kidd in 1961 during the centenary celebrations of their depot in Walmer. Basil would have been at a vantage point on the first floor of Boots the Chemist and his picture shows the modern frontage of Burton's tailors. The New Inn public house, alongside, proudly displays its AA and RAC signs while the junction has acquired traffic lights and road signs. Northey's stationer's, later purchased by John Roper, inset, is shown in the background.

Broad Street – Another view of the Marines parade marking the centenary of the RM depot, Walmer, in 1961. The Basil Kidd picture captures the businesses that were once in Broad Street including, on the left, WH Cullen & Sons corn seed merchants with the Roxborough Castle public house alongside. On the corner of Middle Street is Millicent's sweet shop run by Millicent Butterworth. The premises had earlier been Emma Barber's tearooms, before that Court Lodge Dairy and in 2012 is the Sugar Boy sweet shop. On the right is Nelson House Restaurant that was demolished and is now the site of Deal library. The bay window of Allen's hairdressers can be seen further down on the right and, in the distance, part of Riceman's department store which burnt down in 1963.

Permanent
Waving

MACDONALD
25/-

EUGENE
Genuine Sachets
21/-

OTHER SYSTEMS
From 17/6

A MACDONALD WAVE

ALLEN

Permanent Waving
Specialists

5/7, Broad Street
DEAL

Phone 363

A view of the lower end of Broad Street shows the shops saved from potential demolition and redevelopment planned by Deal Council in the late 1950s. On the left is R Dunn's fruit and vegetable shop which was taken over by John Rayner. Alongside is Charles Thorpe's butcher's, then Jack Allen's ladies' hairdressers and next door his barber's shop. The annexe to South Street Garage was next to Nelson House Café which was on the corner of Middle Street. Whittingham's surplus clothing suppliers can be seen in the distance.

RALEIGH
THE ALL-STEEL CYCLE.

BEWARE OF THE DIRECT FROM THE FACTORY BICYCLE.

Only the "cheapest" class of bicycles are so advertised. "Cheap and nasty" is a well-understood phrase. A Raleigh is truly cheap because its all-steel, scientific construction, and its splendid finish and equipment ensure maximum value for money. 21 years reputation as the best. Prices from **£5 : 19 : 6.** Dunlop tyres, Brooks' saddles, Sturmey Archer 3-speed gear and all the best accessories. *Get the "Book of the Raleigh," post free to any address, and study it.*

"The British Masterpiece."

C. J. LINDSELL,
2 BROAD ST., DEAL.

The staff of Charles Lindsell's cycle shop are pictured outside the premises for a promotional photograph with a variety of cycles and vehicles. The business was on the corner of Broad Street and Middle Street but the building was later demolished for the widening of Broad Street. It is believed the premises were previously Spicer's greengrocers. Inset: A 1912 advertisement for the firm warns against 'cheap and nasty' direct-from-the-factory-bicycles.

Queen Street – The photographer is standing in Queen Street and looking back across the High Street to Broad Street where a policeman is on duty at the junction. On the left is Burton's tailors and the row of shops featured on page 82. On the right are the shops which were subsequently demolished for road widening after a rise in accidents. The business on the right was Mr Inkerman Baker's ham and beef stores, Mr Edward Williams saddle and harness maker's shop and Mr Harry Frank Romney's bakers and confectioners with, as the advertisement on the side of the building shows, teas provided.

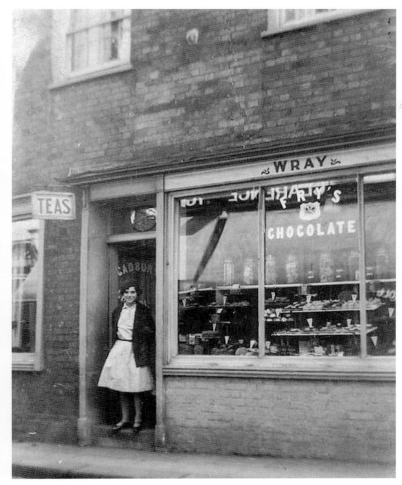

Elsie Shaw, neé Bailey, stands in the doorway of Miss Wray's bakery at 3 High Street. The picture was taken around 1929 when Elsie was 14 and had begun work at the bakers and confectioners. The premises are featured on the opposite page as the earlier business of Mr Inkerman Baker's ham and beef stores but were demolished in the 1930s for road widening.

Left: Across the road Charlie Jenkins is pictured in his fishmongers at 18 Queen Street in the 1960s with a fine display of fish and seafood. Right: A slightly older Charlie at the shop window before the business closed and he joined son Steve at his High Street shop featured on page 42. The Queen Street shop became Teasels Florist and is now Contemporary Flowers.

WORSFOLD & HAYWARD

AUCTIONEERS AND ESTATE AGENTS

ARCHITECTS, SURVEYORS AND VALUERS

21, QUEEN STREET, DEAL

('Phone: Deal 442)

and at DOVER and ST. MARGARET'S-AT-CLIFFE

REGISTER OF PROPERTY FOR SALE AND TO LET

Rents Collected.   Auctions of Property and Furniture
Valuations for all Purposes

Agents for The Guardian Assurance Co., Ltd.

Agents for The Walmer Castle and Upper Deal Estates

A 1934 advertisement for Worsfold & Hayward auctioneers and estate agents shows the frontage of the property at 21 Queen Street. Many people will remember the firm at 11 Queen Street in the 1970s and 1980s, alongside the East Kent Mercury office, and the building is now Deal Discount Domestic.

In 1980 Dover District Council approved a planning application for demolition of Denne's builder's yard, pictured on the left, and the little row of shops alongside. Originally Denne's wanted to build a three storey office block and shops but the plan was withdrawn and a further application was submitted to build Queen's Mews, the complex of warden assisted flats which is now on the site. Among the traders affected by the demolition were Mr and Mrs TH Swift of The Floor Shop, Deal Appliance Centre that had been Mr and Mrs Fowler greengrocer, JB Finn secondhand furniture shop and the English Food Takeaway that had been the office of Minter's Removals.

Reginald Charles Howland, pictured right, with Mr WE Rogers in the doorway of their estate agents, auctioneers and valuers business at 29 Queen Street. The premises are featured on the previous page as The Floor Shop. Mr Howland later carried on the business on his own until World War Two when, like many traders and local families, he moved away. On his return in 1945 Mr Howland opened up in Stanhope Road (see page 131). To the left of the picture is a glimpse of JB Thorpe's sweet shop.

Brian Weeden's photograph taken in 1970 records the once familiar sight of double decker buses at the stop in Queen Street, on this occasion a 1961 AEC Regent. Nicely captured behind is Gregory's Glass, paint and wallpaper shop. The business had previously been in Market Street and later moved to St George's Road behind the town hall. John Gregory ran the firm, followed by his son, also John.

Left: John Gregory senior is pictured in his shop shown on the previous page. Above: A variety of mirrors and other products on display in the first floor showroom of Gregory's Glass in Queen Street. The Queen Street shop had previously been GC Allen & Co auctioneers and estate agents, established in 1878. The shop was taken over by Bryan Wilding in 1975, who had previously worked at Allen's barbers in Broad Street. Bryan retired in 2012 and the property is now The Cutting Room.

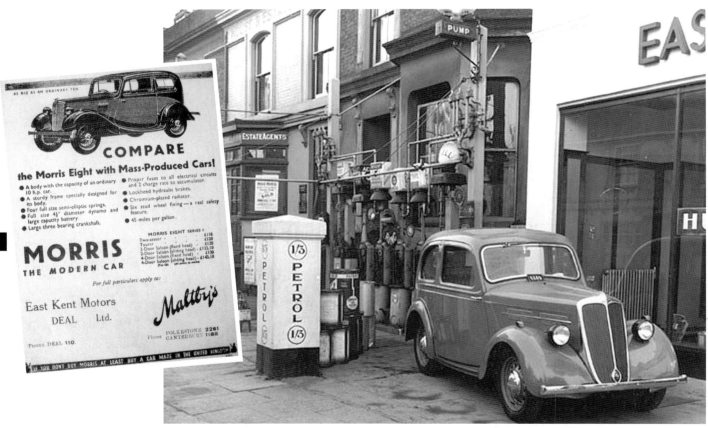

East Kent Motors was at 49 Queen Street, on the corner of Blenheim Road, and is pictured in 1935. It became Caffyn's Garage and is now a Kwik-Fit tyre centre. On the left of the picture is GW Finn estate agents, valuers and auctioneers. The firm became Honeyball & Finn when the two firms merged in 1937.

Petrol was 1s 3d per gallon (about 7p) when this photo of East Kent Motors and its petrol pumps was taken in 1935.

Bill Follett with his wife Mary, right, and sister-in-law Jo Marriott, stand outside Follett's Café with one of their magnificent displays of hanging baskets and boxes promoting the plants they also sold. Mary died in the late 1990s but in 2000, when most people would have retired, Jo, and Bill who was then 80, closed the café and

opened Deal Garden Centre. Bill and Jo finally retired in 2009 and the business still operates as Deal Garden Centre. Right: Bill Follett outside the shop on his retirement aged 89.

Vic and Brenda Baugh at the counter of their café at 48 Queen Street. The couple ran the café during the late 1950s until 1966. Vic had opened the business when Cavell's bakery closed, moving from his hut in the station approach. The premises became Follett's Café and then Deal Garden Centre featured on the previous page. Inset: Vic Baugh pictured outside Vic's Café in the Deal station approach in 1952.

High Street cont – This view of the junction of Queen Street and Deal High Street marks the final section of High Street photographs. Here, the corner shop is shown as Lilley & Skinner's shoe shop which became Mansfield's shoe shop. It had previously been Boots the Chemist before it moved to 39 High Street. Methold's grocers had been on the site before it was demolished to widen the narrow entrance to Queen Street. The gas showrooms can be seen next door.

The Deal & Walmer Gas Company showroom, seen here in 1934, displays the latest in gas appliances including "Cooking, eating, hot water supply, switch controlled lighting and refrigeration." The showroom was at 21a High Street but is now a branch of Starburger. On the left is a glimpse of William Darracott's drapery shop.

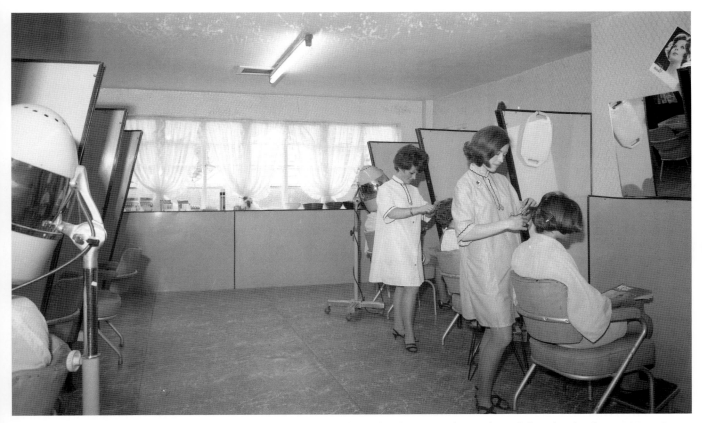

Hair styles change and salon interiors clearly date but these looks were the order of the day in the 1960s when this picture was taken. The photo is thought to show Vogue hairdresser on the first floor above Bowkett's baker's and café and had previously been Rolfe's hairdresser. Bartlett and White fruiterer is on the ground floor of the premises in 2012.

The attractive frontage and impressive gas lamps of the premises featured on the left of the picture belong to Sir William Darracott's shop at 21 High Street. It is listed in Kelly's 1899 Directory as 'family draper, costume and mantle maker, hosier, laceman, milliner, dressmaker and general furnisher & c.' The picture shows the narrow entrance to Queen Street. Inset: Sir William Darracott was a founder of Deal & Walmer Chamber of Commerce and its President in 1909, and Chairman of Victoria Deal, Walmer & District War Memorial Hospital. He was knighted in 1932 for his services to the local community and to the Conservative party.

Right: If only our High Street looked so attractive today. On the left at number eleven, sheltered by the impressive blind, was Fred Franklin's draper's. Next door at number nine was John Franklin, thought to be Fred's brother, selling a wide range of 'fancy drapery' from ribbons to clocks. The firm was established in 1808 by William Franklin.

High Street, Deal.

Left: An internal view of Franklin's fancy draper's, photographed circa 1897, with an impressive line of chairs for customers to sit on while being served.

We owe much to Franklin's Studio, pictured at the bottom of South Street. The firm recorded many local views that are now invaluable local history resources. The picture takes in businesses featured on the previous page and shows Lloyds Bank on the right.

CAVE'S ORIENTAL CAFES

SUPPLY THE SOUTH COAST
:: with their noted ::
Teas and Coffees

AND IN ALL THEIR CAFES FROM
BRIGHTON TO MARGATE (SEE MAP).

They serve Delicious Coffee,
Dainty Afternoon Teas,
and Light Refreshments

NEW BRANCH NOW OPEN!!

24. HIGH STREET, DEAL.

High Street (Looking North), Deal.

In the summer of 1936 a series of East Kent Mercury advertisements announced a new branch of Cave's Oriental Cafés would open at 24 High Street. Sadly, the ornate shop front is long gone. The premises had earlier been Charles Weston's grocery store and, in more recent years, was a branch of the Trustees Savings Bank but is now a betting shop. Alongside Cave's was Page's shoe shop while Timothy White's chemist was on the corner of Broad Street.

The well-stocked and smartly arranged goods are in the windows of Charles Weston & Co 'purveyors of choice teas and high class provisions.' The picture appeared in the first local illustrated directory for Deal and Walmer circa 1897.

Now a branch of Superdrug, 6-10 High Street is captured here by Basil Kidd as a branch of Vyes 'the Kentish grocer.' Previously, the premises had been Peter Comfort's ironmongers and, even earlier, RG Long & Sons boot and shoe makers. Next door can be seen Bateman's opticians which became a branch of Vision Express but closed in 2012. Ashley Brown's jewellery shop was alongside and is now Laines.

The traditional and much missed Peter Comfort's ironmonger's was at 10 High Street, now the site of Superdrug. The firm, founded by Peter's father Percy Comfort, had been located at 90 High Street, opposite St George's Church, and was one of the businesses bombed during World War Two.

Peter Comfort's ironmongers, seen here around 1960 with a smart new shop front displaying the wide variety of tools, equipment and kitchenware which made the shop indispensable. The popular business relocated to Queen Street but closed when Peter and Grace Comfort retired in 1994 and it became Lynda's drugstore.

H. TAYLOR & SON,

SOUTH STREET

AND

WEST STREET.

Every Description of Coal or Coke.

South Street – Once there was a constant stream of buses arriving and departing in South Street with queues of waiting passengers. This 1966 picture by Mike Ansell shows the 84 Mill Hill service bus, a 1950 lowbridge bodied Guy Arab III double decker. To the right is H Taylor & Son coal merchants with King's Toy Shop at the bottom of South Street, on the corner of Wellington Road, and a glimpse of Francis Day photographer.

Mr P Redmond took this photograph in 1960 to record the smart 1948 Dennis Lancet coach. South Street Garage, pictured behind, was run by McCormick and Bourner. On the left can be seen the 'TEAS coffees and ices' sign of the neighbouring South Street Parlour, owned by Anna Varlese from the 1950s until she retired in 1997.

DEAL TELEPHONE, No. 10.

W. SOUTHEY & CO.

Poulterers and Fishmongers, South Street, Deal. . . .

Receive Fresh Supplies Daily of

Turbot.	Brills.	Soles.	Salmon.
Lemon Soles.	Fresh Haddock.	Whitings.	Halibut.
Cod.	Fresh Herrings.	Haddies.	Kippers.
Lobsters.	Crabs.	Shrimps.	Prawns.
Plaice.	Hake.	Bloaters.	Whitstable Oysters.

SURREY FOWLS. CHICKEN. DUCKS. PIGEONS.

ICE SUPPLIED.

Southey & Co fishmonger, poulterer and ice merchant, is shown at 2 South Street. William R Southey owned the business which he later ran with his son William. Edward Drincqbier had previously run his fishmonger's business here which he had acquired from Mr H Waugh in 1875. More recently it was Grigg's fishmongers but is now a branch of the Subway sandwich chain.

William Southey, pictured right, with his staff of Southey & Co fishmongers and a spectacular display of fish and poultry. The picture was taken in the early 1900s when it was the fashion to display produce over the frontage of shops for promotional pictures.

John and Rose Ward are photographed with their assistant on the steps of Rothwell House sweet shop and tobacconist. Technically, the business was at 4 Beach Street but traded from South Street which is where many people will remember buying their seaside buckets, spades and candy floss. Alistair Lawton, former Mayor of Deal, originally opened Rothwell House in the 1950s along with a further shop at 33 High Street. Inset: This 1967 view shows the official entrance in Middle Street and shop frontage in South Street.

Victoria Road – A familiar sight of flooding at the junction of Victoria Road, South Street and High Street. A King & Son, the very popular toy shop, can be seen on the left, on the corner of the High Street and Wellington Road. On the right, on the corner of Sondes Road, is Sharp's Dairy, formerly The Vale Dairy, and, further back, the 'films' and 'chemist' signs of Sharp and Waterhouse chemist. In the distance, a car drives past Woolworth's and a bus turns right into Broad Street, all before pedestrianisation.

As the band of the Royal Marines parades along Victoria Road on the way back to barracks it passes Nicholas Kingsman baker's and café, on the corner of South Street, that was previously the very popular Tapping's bakery. Next door is Sharp and Waterhouse chemist which was previously owned by Edward Dobson, Mayor of Deal from 1939-1944. Franklin's craft shop is alongside and then The Coffee Inn run by Robert and Joyce Stuke. The shop still retains its attractive frontage with art deco style glass windows and leaded lights.

The Strand – Here are two early views of Snow's stationer and newsagent at 45 The Strand, with its attractive wrought iron railings, owned by Mr John William Snow. Frank Hunt, well known as the secretary of Deal, Walmer and Kingsdown Rowing Club, started working for Mr Snow in 1918 and eventually took over the business in 1955 and retired in 1973.

Royal Marines stand to attention on Walmer Green, the occasion recorded by Basil Kidd during the RM centenary celebrations in 1961. The picture captures in the background Frank Hunt's newsagents business at 45 The Strand, and shows the unfurled sunblind with the firm's name emblazoned upon it. Next door is S Hind & Son auctioneers and estate agents, Peter Marriott's opticians, William Boothby's butchers and the Lord Nelson public house on the corner. Hunt's continued as a newsagent and tobacconist, incorporating a sub Post Office after the Lower Walmer Post Office at 38 The Strand, closed. In 2009, the building finally closed as a newsagent and Post Office and is now The Walmer Launderette. Inset: Frank Hunt wearing his Deal Rowing Club blazer.

The sight of Royal Marines parading on Walmer Green is no longer the regular scene it once was. There are many other changes along The Strand including the closure of many shops. Lower Walmer Post Office, seen on the right of the Royal Marines Association Club, was once a thriving, high class establishment with stationery and gifts as well as the all-important Post Office counter service. On the left of the picture is H Symon's greengrocers, also pictured overleaf at a later date.

A tempting display of fruit and vegetables outside Mary and Roger's greengrocers at 32 The Strand. Mary and Roger Steward owned the shop between 1985 and 1990. To the right of the greengrocers is a glimpse of the Royal Marine Association and, on the previous page, both premises are featured with Lower Walmer Post Office.

A busy day on The Strand with Alfred Webber and his men, of 60 The Strand, painting the front of the Alma Tavern. It was later called the Alma Hotel and became a branch of Lloyds Bank before becoming a private house. To the left is William Trigg & Co boot and shoe maker. It became The Green Café, later The Russett and is now The Bandstand Bakery. A laden cart and barrow stand outside Loyns high-class outfitter and draper.

Another busy view of The Strand from the 1920s, this time looking further along. On the left is the newsagent Frederick Giles, still a newsagent, Walmer News, in 2012. The True Briton public house is alongside. This became The Lifeboat Inn, one of the many public houses that have closed on The Strand, leaving only The Stag trading in 2012. Next door are the International Stores and John Tapping's bakery before St Saviour's Church on the right.

Royal Marines return to barracks after the 1961 centenary parade. Basil Kidd's picture was taken from the first floor of the National Provincial Bank at 1 The Beach. John Lukey & Sons wine merchants is seen second building on the left, trading in 2012 as The Strand Wine Co. The stag on the sign next along denotes the name of the pub beneath. L Beaney fruiterer adjoins then Sharp and Waterhouse chemist and Wale & Son ironmongers.

★ *Ford has achieved it* —

The £100

Saloon Car

Ford

" There is no Comparison "

The Popular Ford Saloon (£100 at Works) is no experiment. It is already the world's most famous light car, in keen demand overseas as well as at home, because of its outstanding performance and its matchless dependability. Let us demonstrate.

R. E. GOOCH, Walmer Garage.   Phone: Deal 149.

Dover Road and Upper Walmer – Walmer Garage, on the corner of Cambridge Road, is decorated for a celebration. As the advertisement shows, the garage became Ronald Gooch's Garage and then Gooch & Jones. It had formerly been WH Wyborn's Garage and Cycle shop and previously the Wellesley Arms public house. It is now Maurice and Mark Green's Carpet Centre.

Studio.

W. A SAWYER,
PHOTOGRAPHIC ARTIST

William Sawyer's photographic studio shows the range of backdrops and props used for studio portraits and photographs. William Sawyer's home and studio were at Westfield House, Dover Road, pictured below.

Sawyer's home was close to Walmer Nursery, now replaced with a more modern house. William was the son of Willard Sawyer, pioneering manufacturer of the velocipede, an early form of bicycle. Willard moved from Dover to 8 St George's Road, then St George's Place, and it is now the Deal Maritime and Local History Museum. Here he continued in business and his son William started as a photographer. Later, they moved to Dover Road where William continued working as a photographer until around 1914.

A flag flies atop the art deco style showroom of Henlys Garage on Dover Road in the 1960s when a secondhand Austin Cambridge could be bought for £420. Earlier, the business had been County Motors (Kent) Limited. The smart showroom was demolished and in 2012 the site, at the corner of Salisbury Road, is Walmer Adamsons Motors Limited and the Esso petrol station. Walmer Village Hall, which opened in 1912, is on the right, its side elevation and windows on show before alteration of the garage forecourt obscured the view.

This scene shows a more tranquil Dover Road, Upper Walmer, compared to the busy main road of today. On the left is the George & Dragon public house, now the Thompson's Bell. Alongside is the Walmer branch of Vye & Son 'the Kentish grocer' which had branches in Queen Street and Deal High Street. A lone car is parked outside Harry Pickard's butcher's shop. Further along, on the corner of Station Road, was Farmer's grocery stores run by Mrs Florence Farmer which became a branch of J Lukey & Sons wine merchants and is now a Londis store.

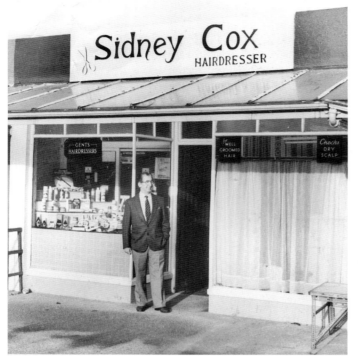
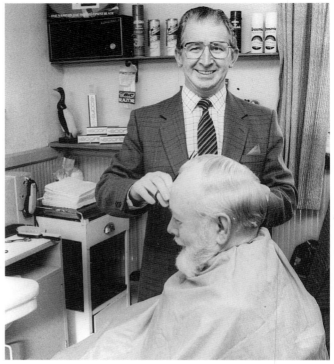

Around the town – Sid Cox was a popular barber and is pictured outside his shop at 10 Park Avenue, and with a customer, in the late 1970s. Sid was born in 1914 and was working for Frank Sillitoe, tailor, of South Court, when one day a workmate needed a haircut. Sid obliged with his tailoring shears which led to his idea of becoming a barber. Sid was a Walmer Sea Scouts leader and practised haircuts on the scouts for 1d a time. In 1936, against all advice, he took on the Park Avenue premises for 12s 6d (63p) a week charging 6d for men and 4d for boys. Sid would put a plank of wood across the seat to make it high enough for children. He was Chairman of Walmer Sea Scouts for 25 years and a life Vice President of Deal Town Football Club. Sid died aged in 2008 aged 94.

It seems unbelievable an attractive shop such as William Dunn's florist, fruiter and greengrocer at 79 West Street, could be demolished along with its nursery and greenhouses, but that is the case. The former business is now the site of the St George's car park and the large size of the premises is clearly shown on the 1911 Ordnance Survey map. Louisa Emily Dunn, granddaughter of the owner William, is pictured in the doorway of the shop. The family closed the business and moved to Staple during World War Two and the building was later knocked down.

William Dunn, left, born 1849, with his sons Frederick and Frederick Edward are pictured in the 1920s outside the greenhouse of Portland Nurseries, part of the business of William Dunn florist, fruiterer, greengrocer and nurseryman at 79 West Street, pictured on the previous page. A first prize certificate can be glimpsed through the window among the flowers and plants.

The smart grocery shop Stanhope Stores was on the corner of Stanhope Road and West Street. More recently the building was used by Goldcrest estate agents until that closed in 2009 and in 2012 stood empty. Stanhope Stores was owned by William 'Bill' and Daphne Abel between 1950 and 1955 and later by D McBeth. Previously, Bill had been manager of Vyes the grocer in their High Street shop.

"Would madam like it delivered?" An internal view of a quintessential British grocer's shop shows Stanhope Stores open for business in the early 1950s. William 'Bill' Abel, his wife Daphne and staff attend to a smartly dressed customer. Their advertisement boasted "Grocery and provisions, beer, wines and spirits. We collect and deliver orders."

Howland & Co estate agents is pictured at 1 Stanhope Road, now Deal Rental Bureau premises. Reginald Charles Howland had originally been in business in Queen Street (see page 89) but, like many firms, closed and moved away during World War Two. In 1945 he returned and opened at Stanhope Road where he was later joined in the business by his son John. Mr Howland retired in 1978, aged 72, when John Ludlum estate agent took over the premises.

J & E Rogers' bakery is pictured at 2 Church Path, on the corner of Albert Road, photographed between 1958 and 1963. John and his wife Betty took over the premises in 1955, moving their bakery from North Street, where they still retained a shop until the early 1970s. They retired in 1985 closing their businesses in Church Path, 132 High Street and 22 King Street, Sandwich. The Church Path premises were earlier a Post Office and bakery run by Arthur and Mary Kingsford and is now D & L Homecare.

Right: John Rogers is pictured at the ovens of his bakery in Albert Road which was behind the shop featured on the previous page. Left: John Rogers at work decorating one of the many Christmas and wedding cakes he produced over the decades. In 2012 and aged 95, John still makes his own bread every week with the help of son Michael.

Upper Deal – This early picture shows the London Road and Manor Road junction with the posts of the old tollgate in the foreground. On the left is the old single storey building that still stands today which was Alf Doughty's shoe repairer's for many years. The Liverpool Arms is alongside and Admiral Keppel further on. This junction was known as Parker's Corner for many years after Stephen Parker ginger beer manufacturer who lived at Jenkins Well at one time and 'farmed' the tolls.

Above: An advertisement for Parker's ginger beer from the Deal, Walmer and Sandwich Mercury dated 1889 showing the firm was established in 1852. Stephen Parker was born in Northbourne in 1819 and died in 1916 aged 97. His funeral was carried out by Stephen Mockett builder and undertaker of Upper Deal (featured on page 138). Below: An early cod bottle engraved 'Stephen Parker ginger beer manufacturer.'

Right: At the mention of the shops in Upper Deal, people will often recall Doughty's shoe repair shop and the smell of glue and leather. This photograph shows Alf Doughty at his work bench with scraps of leather at his feet. Above: Alf Doughty's shoe repair shop on the corner of Manor Road and London Road, pictured around 1970. The building still exists, although now sadly neglected. In the top left hand corner of the picture is a tantalising glimpse of the roof of Warden House School.

Holly Cottage was in London Road at Upper Deal and the home of Stephen Mockett & Son, builder, contractor and undertaker whose workshops were at the side of the building. Sadly, the cottage was demolished around 1970 and is now the site of two houses that lay back from the road at numbers 292 and 294.

138

Left: Stephen Mockett is pictured in his garden at Holly Cottage, 294 London Road, Upper Deal. Right: An attractive invoice for funeral expenses from Stephen Mockett, builder, contractor and undertaker dated 1913. It is probable that an old invoice was in use as, by this date, Stephen's son Perce (1889-1972) had joined the firm.

Stephen Mockett stands in his builder's yard behind Holly Cottage, Upper Deal. His works vehicle is on the right and, what appears to be, the body of an old Ford on the left – perhaps they originally went together? Stephen was born in 1862 and died in 1939 aged 77.

Many people remember St Leonard's Cycle Works, or Upper Deal cycle shop as it was commonly called, at St Leonard's Terrace. Ebenezer and Laura Walder owned the shop in the 1940s. Laura is pictured, right, with her daughter Mrs Daphne Abel and granddaughter Sandy. Later Mr and Mrs C Killick owned the shop. St Leonard's Terrace was once thriving with the bakery started by Harry Chitty in the 1800s and continued by Mark Goodchild today. Next door was Stan Elgar, barber, Mrs Firrell's wool shop and then the cycle shop. Mr and Mrs G Lane had Upper Deal Post Office and Mr Taylor took over the tobacconist and sweet shop in the next building.

Middle Deal Road

This postcard shows the Upper Deal and Middle Deal Road junction with Eythorne Cottage on the left. There was a small corner shop at the far end of the terrace, on the right, and the forge beyond. The shop was run by butcher Walter Heritage in 1915 and AJ Harris Mayes in 1936 before becoming a grocery shop. In the foreground, on the right, is the hedging that used to border the flowerbed which still exists today. But it is the enterprising advertisement for Lindsell's Garage that catches the eye.

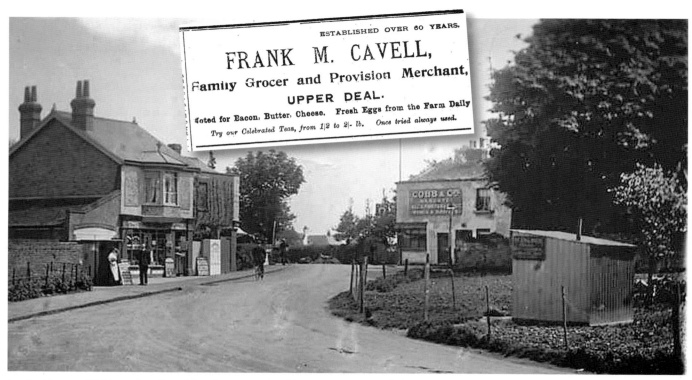

ESTABLISHED OVER 60 YEARS.

FRANK M. CAVELL,

Family Grocer and Provision Merchant,

UPPER DEAL.

Noted for Bacon, Butter, Cheese. Fresh Eggs from the Farm Daily

Try our Celebrated Teas, from 1/2 to 2/- lb. Once tried always used.

Leslie House, 224 London Road, is photographed here as a general shop thought to be run by Mr and Mrs Ovenden, pictured outside. Billboards carry headlines of the Kaiser's downfall in World War One. Colin Stokes, who runs The Roast House B&B, which was previously a teashop, dates the building from 1901. Within a few years it had become a general store, later Peter Harris-Mayes' butcher's shop and then 'the pet shop' run by John Le Lacheur. Next door is the vine covered wall of Vine House which was a grocery shop and Post Office run by Frank Cavell. Later, it was a branch of the Co-op and then Gilling's antique shop. Opposite, the Magnet Inn is shown before the dairy and butcher's shop were built alongside. Inset: A 1912 advertisement for Frank Cavell's grocer's shop.

Doing the rounds – Market gardener and well-known local character Cedric 'Curly' Friend holding his grand-daughter Sarah at Sandwich Market in 1975, pictured with his prize winning turkeys. Curly was renowned for seldom wearing a shirt even in the coldest weather and famously remembered for dumping a trailer load of dirt at the entrance to Deal railway station in 1974 during a dispute with British Rail.

A picture from a bygone age shows a young Curly Friend in his pram in 1920 on the fields of his parents' market garden at North Deal. Pictured with the horse-drawn plough are his father Harry Garibaldi, mother Mary Anne and his sisters.

Bill Nash, pictured right, was the chimney sweep everyone called upon in the days when most houses were coal fired. He was a projectionist at the Odeon Cinema in Queen Street and began sweeping chimneys in 1954 before finally retiring aged 69. Bill won a contract for 7s 6d (37.5p) to sweep chimneys at the Royal Marines depot, Walmer, and was still working there 10 years later. He died in February 2011, aged 82, and was married to Betty who still lives at the family home where they brought up eight children.

Henry 'Harry' Thomsett, who first established Thomsett's Coaches in 1929 and at that time lived with his family at 16 Dolphin Street, is pictured standing in Alfred Square alongside the firm's first bus, a Morris Commercial, circa 1938. He was able to buy the vehicle after pit baths were installed at Betteshanger colliery and clean miners could be transported home after their shift in comparative comfort!

Prior to buying the bus featured opposite, Harry had purchased a Morris Commercial lorry, circa 1929, in hope of transporting miners to and from Betteshanger colliery. Business took off and soon Harry was also delivering the miners' concessionary coal to their homes with the same vehicle. Benches were put across the back of the lorry for the men to sit on and between shifts these were removed for carrying the coal.

A 1950 Dennis coach, pictured soon after purchase in early 1965 by Thomsett's from East Kent, was a familiar sight around Deal and district. Thomsett's coaches were also used for taking hop pickers to and from the hop gardens, transporting children to and from school as well as private hire – including their very popular country drives.

Three generations of the Thomsett family, photographed in the 1970s, with one of their coaches. They are, from left to right: Sidney, still in charge in 2012, Alf Craker, brother-in-law to brothers Jack, Jim and Sid Thomsett who are standing behind their mother, Harriet Eliza. Father Harry died in 1942, aged 57, so widow Harriet kept the firm going until her sons returned from the Second World War.

Above: A Neal & Son lorry, circa 1962. Around 1960 Albert and his brother George Neal had opened Neal Brothers Auction Room and Removals at 104 Middle Street, closing when Albert died in 1966. Albert had been a general porter from around 1953 using his barrow to transport goods. Right: Albert's son Terry is pictured with Les Coe (back to camera) who worked at the removal firm before joining Job's Furniture Store. When the business closed Terry owned boats on the seafront and organised pleasure trips. Later, he started up a coach and vehicle self-hire business and now runs RT Tours with his wife Ruby.

James Pitcher, who lived at 6 Rutland Terrace, Northwall Road, Deal, was a coal deliveryman for Hoare, Gothard & Bond (Dover) Ltd, coal merchants. He is pictured in May 1924 with the firm's horse and cart, possibly at their Deal depot, believed to be near Denne's Yard in Queen Street. James, who was born in 1885, later set up his own coal merchant's business run from 86 Northwall Road, with the coal yard behind Rutland Terrace. When he retired in 1951, James handed over the business to his sons Arthur 'Dick' and William 'Bill.' Bill carried on with the firm when Dick died until he then retired in 1978.

Christopher Terry, coal merchant and carrier, stands proudly with his coal laden horse and cart outside the Queen Adelaide Inn, Church Street, Walmer, in 1902. Christopher, born 1876, lived with his wife Elizabeth and two sons in Waterworks Road, now St Richard's Road, Deal.

William Robert Minter, like many businessmen of his day, did a variety of jobs including that of fly proprietor (a type of cart), carrier, coal and coke merchant. He was licensee of The Drum public house, where he stands outside, opposite Walmer Castle Road, at 203 Dover Road, Upper Walmer, before it was demolished.

George Wells Woodcock, born 1849, had a grocer's shop at 333 Dover Road, Upper Walmer. Frederick Charles Woodcock worked with his father before setting up on his own in Lawn Road to grow sweet peas where his son Austin Frederick joined him and later took over the business. The family had other shops in Dover Road and Downs Road. Family member Jack Woodcock is pictured, right, in Walmer Castle Road, with the firm's delivery bicycle inscribed 'FC Woodcock, high class fruiterer, Walmer.'

Left: EA Woodcock's greengrocer and confectioner at the Station Road end of Court Road owned by another brother Edwin Arthur.

Left: Charles 'Pop' Cage, 65 year old bakery delivery boy, outside Rogers the bakers of North Street, Deal. Pop, father of Mrs Rogers, delivered bread in the North Deal area for the family firm.

Right: Frank Catt, born 1918, as a 19 year old on a firm's bicycle and cart with the logo 'Catt's Restaurant, noted for steak and kidney pies, fresh daily.'

Above: An illustration of John Pittock's furniture delivery van. The highly regarded business was at 49-53 High Street and once boasted furniture and drapery as well as gentlemen's and ladies' outfitters departments.

Right: Jim Ashby, delivery boy for Maxted's Petshop, when at 134 High Street, Deal, pictured on the firm's bicycle.

Left: A Jobs of Deal furniture van – a Luton bodied Ford Transit. Job's furniture store was in West Street, now part of the Sainsbury's supermarket site, and was run by Maurice Job and begun by his grandfather Stapleton Willey Job.

Right: A van, probably an Austin, belonging to Solley's Mongeham Farm Dairy of Great Mongeham, promoting pasteurised milk on the sides.

Left: A delivery to Mrs Maude Cory, at Lea House, Princes Street, Deal, from a Vyes delivery vehicle. At one time Vyes had branches in Deal and Walmer and many more across the county.

Right: William James 'Billie' Hancock and his mother-in-law Mrs Florence Newing with his builder's lorry. Hancock's yard was in Gladstone Road, Walmer.

Right: Deal Beach Parlour's ice cream vans brought joy to thousands of children over the years.

Below: This impressive line up of Lambert's Laundry motor and horse drawn vehicles was featured in 'Town and Country News' in July 1932. The article praises the business that was in Northwall Road. "... Known for its thoroughly good work in all departments. There is a staff of 100 there, all the girls beginning there are 14. There are fine open-air drying grounds where the fine, ozone-laden air, for which Deal is famous, is able to do its work. When weather conditions do not permit outdoor drying, the latest type of drying machine is used."

Bibliography

Deller, Julie (1993) Bygone Kent. Vol 14, number 12.
East Kent Mercury – various editions.
Glover, S and Rogers, M (2010) Old Pubs of Deal and Walmer. Bygone Publishing.
http://freespace.virgin.net/andrew.parkinson - Northbourne Sources
Rochard, JS Deal, Walmer and Sandwich illustrated (c1897) Gravesend.
Town and Country News 22nd July 1932
www.dovermuseum.co.uk

I am indebted to Michael Rogers for proof-reading and all his help and to Charles Finn for all his continued help and support.

Reproduction of photographs and material: Once again I am grateful to Nick Kidd for generously allowing me the use of Basil Kidd's photographs. Also many thanks to the following people who lent me photographs: the late Mrs Daphne Abel, Mike Ansell, Jim Ashby, David Chamberlain, Les Coe, Peter Comfort, Heather Corley, Mrs Betty Day, Julie Deller, Michael and Shirley Divito, Ruth Doughty, Bill Follett, Alan Ford, Andy Friend, Sheila Fuggle, John Gregory, Kathleen Horton, John Howland, Charlie and Steve Jenkins, Andrea Johnson, Rosemary Johnson, Waveney Jordan, Jerry Laker, Andrew Lomax, Stephen Mockett, Mary Morey, Betty Nash, Terry Neal, Malcolm and Pam Norman, Mrs Hilda Pitcher, Mr P Redmond, John Rogers, Michael Rogers, John Roper, Sylvia Sear, Mrs Elsie Shaw, Susan Smith, David and Susan Solley, Ron Southey, Chris and Colin Spicer, Mary and Roger Steward, Mr Jim Thomsett, Pat Thomsett-Jones, Cynthia Tucker, Ann Vowles, John Ward, Brian Weeden, Bryan Wilding, the Wilson family, Mr R Wilson, Frances Woodcock, Kenneth Woods.

The following organisations generously allowed me reproduction of photographs: Centre for Kentish Studies, Deal Library staff for use of Vyse Collection, Vyse family, English Heritage, Graham Smith Editor East Kent Mercury, Judges of Hastings Limited.

Thank you to the following people for their help: Bill and Sue Ashby, Johnny Baker, Christian Ball, Sue Briggs Chief Reporter East Kent Mercury, Alan Buckman Addelam History Research Group, Olga Calder, Les Coe, Bert and Georgina Curling, Garry Dickinson, Phil Drake, Chris Gray, Maureen Gee, Simon Howes, Peter Jull and the staff of Zoom Photos, High Street, Deal, Roy Knowles, David and Susan Latham, Adrian Lead, Anne Richie, Claire Steward, Colin Stokes, Zoe Tull, Judy Wilson.

Finally, thank you to Nick Evans for producing this book and patiently dealing with my alterations and additions.

Acknowledgements